Canada

Chelsea Kong

© 2024-2025 Chelsea Kong

All rights reserved. All images used in this book are licensed copies from their respectful owners including Freepik, Ghetty Images, Canva, others. This book or any portion thereof may not be reproduced or used in any manner whatsoever without the express written permission of the publisher except for the use of brief quotations in a book review.

Printed in 2024-2025, Made in Toronto, Canada
ISBN: 978-1-998335-11-4
Library and Archives Canada

Canada is shines from sea to shining sea.
It has many beautiful and nice places to see.
There are lots of things to do.

The Canadian flag became official in 1892. In 1921, King George V gave Canada the Royal Arms and the shield of Canada's new official coat of arms on the Canadian Red Ensign.

There were thousands of designs made. Three Canadians who had the best designs. Pearson Pennant was one of the best.

There were 15 people making the new design.
The Canadian flag was changed a few times.

THE LAND WE CALL OUR HOME

George Stanley's flag was made official on January 28, 1965, by Queen Elizabeth II. Canada celebrated it on February 15, 1965. In 1967, Canada had its 100th birthday.

WINDSOR, ONTARIO

Detroit Skyline

Bright Lights

Peace Fountain

Ambassador Bridge

Windsor is a city in southern Ontario.
It is across from Detroit.
It is at the border of Canada.

LONDON
ONTARIO

It is a city in southwestern Ontario.
You can the VIA Rail and GoTrain there.

Toronto is Ontario's largest cities.
CN Tower, Ripley's Aquarium,
Casa Loma, Royal Ontario Museum, a copy of the parliament building, and more.

NIAGARA FALLS

Niagara Falls is a famous place to visit.
You can ride a boat to see the falls.
It is beautiful at night with all the colours.
There is a Botanical Garden.

OTTAWA

This is the capital city of Canada.
The parliament is here.
The government makes laws here.
It has the Royal Canadian Mounty Police.

KINGSTON

It was going to be the capital city.
It has a river canal.
There is a nice park with an old train.
The famous 1000 island boat ride.

Owensound

It has a beautiful waterfall called Inglis Falls.
You can take a walk and explore more.
They have colourful buildings.

Muskoska

Algonquin Park, Arrowhead Park, and more. A great place with beautiful hiking trails. You can camp, kayak, and canoe.

Explore
NORTH BAY

You can visit the Duschesnay Falls.
They have the Farmer's Market at the harbour.
There is a bicycle bath called Kate Pace Way.

Vancouver, British Columbia

See Canada Place, the Vancouver Skyline, Science World, Stanley Park, Lions Gate Bridge, Vancouver Art Gallery, Gastown, and Harbour Centre.

VICTORIA, BRITISH COLUMBIA

Butchart Gardens is famous in Victoria.
Craigdarroch Castle and see the whales.
You can see the Parliament buildings.
Check out Fisherman's Wharf and Chinatown

Enjoy the sky tram in British Columbia.
There are beautiful mountains and lakes.
It has a beautiful ocean view.

ALBERTA

These are beautiful lakes in Alberta.
You should see the Canadian Rockies.
There are other lakes in Canada to visit.
You can hike, use kayaks, canoes, and boats.

Winnipeg, Manitoba

They have a large football stadium.
The Royal Canadian Mint is where
Canada's coins are made.
Royal Aviation Museum of Western Canada

Quebec City

Quebec has a snow castle.
It is nice to visit the old town Quebec City.
Old Quebec City has a beautiful view.

Quebec

Jacques Cartier National Park

Chelsea

Here are more places to visit in Quebec.

FREDERICTON NEW BRUNSWICK

King's Landing is a place to learn history. They also have maple syrup every year. There are fun things to do in winter.

St. John's Newfoundland

Take a visit to Signal Hill with a nice view.
You can go whale watching.
They have 3 beaches at the coastlines.

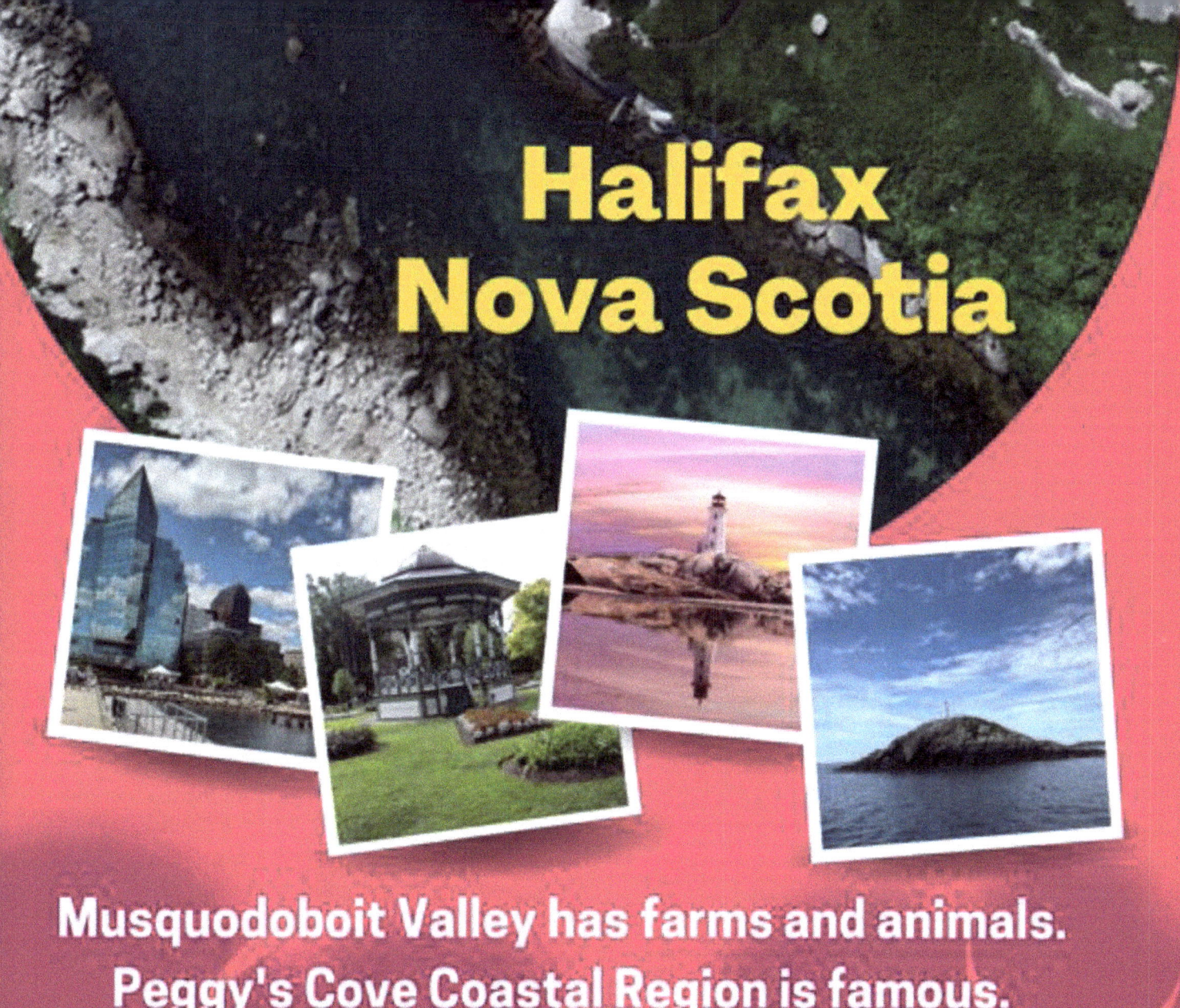

Halifax Nova Scotia

Musquodoboit Valley has farms and animals. Peggy's Cove Coastal Region is famous. Build a sandcastle or surf at the Eastern Shore.

Charlottetown
Prince Edward Island

Charlottetown has a nice view. The confederation bridge is built in the water.

Yellowknife, North West Territories

You can see the beautiful Northern Lights. Enjoy the winter castle, fun on a dogsled, snowshoeing, skiing, and tobogganing. See lakes, trails, and community events.

WHITEHORSE, YUKON

See Emerald Lake and the Northern Lights. Skagway Shore, the Suspension Bridge, Miles Canyon, Beringia Interpretive Centre, and Yukon Transportation Museum.

NUNAVUT

Arctic Bay

Baffin Island

Auyuittuq

Nunavut is the most north place in Canada. Nunavut has 12 places you can visit. You should go to Auyuittuq National Park. You can snowmobile, birdwatch, dogsled, and kayak.

MORE TO SEE

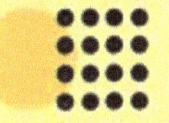

Jasper, Manitoulin Island, Vancouver Island, Yoho, Kootenay, Waterton Lakes and, Whistler, Rideau Canal, Prairies, Bay of Fundy, Churchill, and Drumheller.

VIA Rail

VIA Rail goes from Kingston to Windsor.
It also travels across Canada.
You can take from British Columbia
and travel to Quebec.

Flixbus

Flixbus in Canada only travels in British Columbia, Alberta, and Ontario. It is a global bus you take.

Family Day

Canada celebrates Family Day on the third Monday of the month of February. On October 12, 2007, it was made an official holiday.

VICTORIA DAY

Canada celebrates Victoria Day every third Monday of May. It was named after Queen Victoria.

Civic Holiday

Some provinces in Canada celebrate it is the first Monday of August. Only Nunavut and North West Territories officially calls it Civic Holiday.

It is the first Monday of September. This holiday to honour people who work and labour laws which Canada and USA celebrate.

HAPPY thanksgiving

It is celebrated the third Monday in October. New Brunswick, Nova Scotia, and Prince Edward Island don't celebrate it. Canada used to eat different foods too.

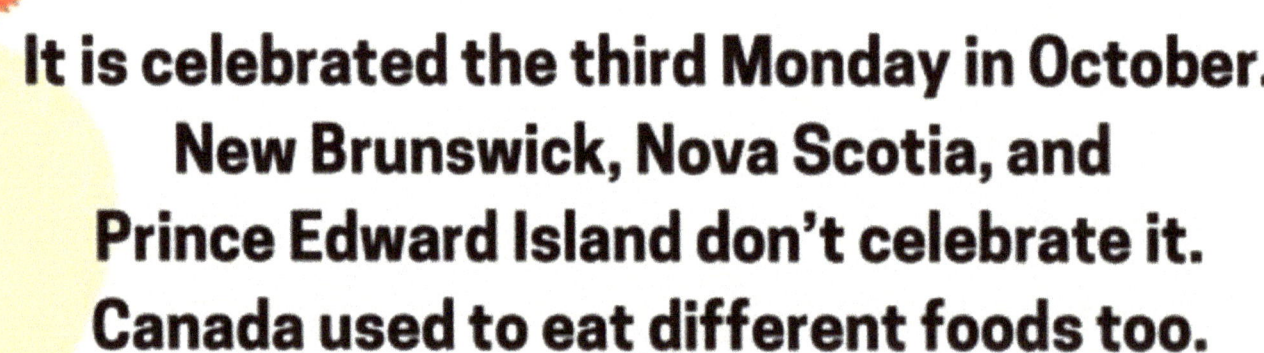

Canada has a great destiny.
It will bring healing to the nations.
It is giving food and more to help others.

Canada will have great churches. It will send missionaries to the world. People will hear about Jesus Christ.

Toronto and Hamilton will be like hot lava. Many people will come into God's family. It is a great revival that will touch Canada.

**The nations of the world will be changed.
Canada will start the revival.
Jesus will return at God's time.**

The nation will bring glory to God.
God's glory will show to His people.
Revival will come from the Chinese.

Revival will come from the Chinese.
People will see God's power.
Churches, work, schools, businesses,
prisons, and the government will change.

**Canada will be full of love and God's fire.
Canada must live for God.
God needs our money, businesses,
homes, and us to do His work.**

WORSHIP

God's people will need to put God first. Spend more time in prayer and the Bible. God will use Canada in the last days.

A mighty army of people in God will rise.
Children and youth will do great things.
Families will become strong and full of love.

References

Government of Canada, "The History of the National Flag of Canada" Government of Canada, 2024. https://www.canada.ca/en/canadian-heritage/services/flag-canada-history.html

Lonely Planet, "15 of the Best Places to Visit in Canada" Lonely Planet, 2024. https://www.lonelyplanet.com/articles/best-places-to-visit-in-canada

Arctic Kingdom, "Explore Qikiqtarjuaq, Nunavut" Arctic Kingdom, 2024. https://arctickingdom.com/destination/qikiqtarjuaq/

References

Destination Nunavut, "Qikiqtarjuaq" Destination Nunavut, 2024. https://destinationnunavut.ca/destinations/qikiqtaaluk-region/qikiqtarjuaq

BillyeBrim Canada, "Prophecies of Canada." BillyeBrim Canada, 2024 https://www.billyebrimcanada.com/canadian-prophecies/

SALVATION PRAYER

God, I know I sinned against you. Forgive me for the wrong that I have done. I believe that Jesus Christ died on the cross for me. That He rose from the grave so that after three days. I can have His long-lasting life. Come into my heart to be my Lord and Savior. I choose to turn away from my sins and I choose to follow you. Lead me to walk with you. Keep me safe and teach me your ways. Stop every bad thing in my life that has an open door to hurt me. Close those doors. Holy Spirit, fill me now in Jesus' name. Amen.

BAPTISM IN THE HOLY SPIRIT

Jesus, you are the one that fills me with Your Spirit. Come Holy Spirit and come into my life and fill me to overflow with Your presence. Come with your fire too. Thank you for the gift of tongues in Jesus' name. Amen.

Open your mouth and let the words come out that God gives you. It will be words that you don't know what they mean. You can ask God what it means. You need to let Him talk through you every day to grow this gift.

He will bring you closer to God and you will know Jesus more. You will have power from God to do great things and know things.

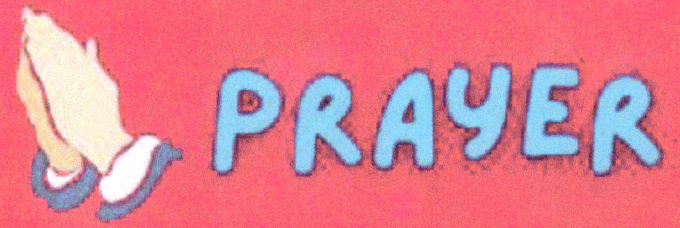# PRAYER

Thank you, Father God, for this book on Canada. I want to be part of the revival that is coming. Bless Canada to walk in your plan. Protect Canada. Make them wise. Teach them your ways. Show me how to share Jesus with others. Holy Spirit change Canada. Tear down the walls that block Canada from knowing you. I pray for the right people to lead Canada. Make her a blessing for you in Jesus' name. Amen.

Message from the Author

Thank you for reading this book. I hope you can leave a good review to encourage me to write more books to teach children and adults. There are so many places in Canada that you can visit that are not in this book. Some places you should go are St. Jacob's, Lake Simcoe, Cobourg, and Thunder Bay. Tecumseh is a nice town and Guelph is a nice city. Remembrance Day is not an official holiday in Canada. Some people get the day off when it is on a weekday. Canada is saved for God's great work. He will use Canada on the days to come. It has blessed by God to change the world. God has a great work for you to do too. He wants us to share Jesus with everyone.

OTHER PRODUCTS

- Knowing God
- How to Hear God's Voice
- New Life in Jesus
- Loving Israel
- God's Gifts/Spiritual Talents
- Meeting God
- Word Power
- Fruit of the Spirit
- The Tabernacle
- Bride for Jesus
- A Life of Prayer
- Live Free
- Who am I in Jesus
- Walk in Love
- God's Favor
- Man of God
- Woman of God
- How to Use Money
- God's Wisdom
- Fasting
- See Jerusalem and Bethany
- First Fruit Offering
- Feast of Trumpets
- Day of Atonement
- Feast of Tabernacles
- Counting the Omer
- Festival of Lights
- Glory, Presence, and Holy Spirit
- Live in God's Presence
- Pentecost
- See Galilee, Nazareth, and Tiberias
- Hear God Speak
- Knowing Jesus
- Knowing Holy Spirit
- A Healthy Life and Healthy Life Work Book
- Smokey the Cat
- Passover Unleavened Bread
- Resurrection Life
- The Blessing
- Revival
- Chelsea Learns Hebrew
- Thanksgiving
- Give Thanks
- Jesus Birth
- Loving Jesus: Bride and Groom
- Proverbs 31 Woman

OTHER PRODUCTS

ABC of People in the Bible
Colours in the Bible
Breakthroughs
Open Doors
The Seven Spirits of God
Numbers in the Bible
Aglee the Eagle
An Eagle's Life
Chelsea Learns Numbers in Hebrew
ABC's of Faith
Feast of Purim
A Royal Life
Pandas
Worship
Fun in the Caribbean

Devotionals
31 Day Devotional

Inspirational/Other
Chelsea's Psalms and Poems
Your Daily Meal: Chelsea's Photo Album
Chelsea's Psalms and Poems2
Travel West Caribbean

Puzzle Books
Biblical Puzzle Book Vol 1-5
Bible Puzzles for Young Children Book 1-3
Biblical Puzzle for Children Books 1-5

OTHER PRODUCTS

Teaching Series

How to Hear God's Voice Teaching Guide & Audio Book

Relationship with God, Jesus, Holy Spirit Guide

Knowing God, Jesus, Holy Spirit Guide & Audio Book

Flowing in the Prophetic

Teaching (Non-Sale on my website)

Purim

Passover

Resurrection

BOOK REVIEWS

More books on Amazon, Kobo, and Barnes and Noble, Smashwords, and IngramSpark.
https://chelseak532002550.wordpress.com/

More books on Amazon, Kobo, and Barnes and Noble, Smashwords, and IngramSpark.
https://www.amazon.com/author/chelseakong

Please leave a review and share with friends to help the author continue to write more books to reach more readers. Thank you so much for your support.

Review!

About
CHELSEA KONG

She is a writer, creative arts and digital media artist, skilled administration and certified PCP (Payroll Compliance Professional), and podcaster. Chelsea also served in a variety of roles, from audiovisual, photography, to assisting on the worship team, and ministry team. She also has a passion for families being united.

Chelsea has been a guest on Unity Live Radio, The Lady Tracey Show, and How to Live for Christ and is highly recommended by a Proud Christian blog. She is also a guest blogger. A few of her books have been featured in YourAuthorHub, etc. She graduated from Hotel and Restaurant Management, Digital Media Arts, Office Administration, Payroll Compliance Professional, and experience working with children. Chelsea lives in Toronto, Canada. She mainly writes children's books, stories, bridal writing, poems, lyrics for songs, words of encouragement, blessings, prayers, and jokes. The author of How to Hear the Voice of God, the Bridal Collection, Knowing God, etc. She also has her own Bible Puzzle books and other inspired products. Her podcast channel is called Chelsea K on Anchor, Spotify, and iTunes.

Please check my website to find out more:
https://chelseak532002550.wordpress.com/

www.ingramcontent.com/pod-product-compliance
Lightning Source LLC
Chambersburg PA
CBHW061356010526
44107CB00012B/957